A Girl's Guide to

MONEY

A Girl's Guide to

MONEY

Make the Rent, Control Your Credit Cards, Afford a Car, Pay Your Mobile Bill,
and Still Have Money for Shopping Sprees and Nights on the Town

Laura Brady

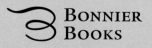

Bonnier
Books

First published in the UK 2007
by Bonnier Books

Bonnier Books
Appledram Barns
Birdham Road
Chichester
PO20 7EQ
Bonnier Books website:
www.bonnierbooks.co.uk

ISBN-13: 978-1-905825-47-9

Conceived and created by
Axis Publishing Limited
8c Accommodation Road
London NW11 8ED
www.axispublishing.co.uk

Creative Director: Siân Keogh
Art Director: Clare Reynolds
Editorial Director: Anne Yelland
Illustrations: Marie Simpson
Production Manager: Jo Ryan

9 8 7 6 5 4 3 2 1

Printed and bound in China

a girl's guide to money

contents

introduction   6

chapter one
bank on it!   8

chapter two
control yourself   30

chapter three
shop until you stop   58

chapter four
now voyager   82

chapter five
rescue remedy   98

chapter six
the future starts now   124

index   142

introduction

*D*ealing with money is something that everyone needs help with, but this guide has been written strictly with girls in mind.

Although it's great to live in an age where females can be self-sufficient, this also means earning enough money to pay our own taxes, bills and mortgages. Us girls also live independently which – single or not – means going out with our own friends. But of course this also means spending money in bars, restaurants and cinemas.

We are lucky to have the option of around-the-clock shopping, but this also means we are faced with more temptation than ever before to spend money.

Getting access to what you want is also easier than ever: you can wear today, pay tomorrow. But this shopping method means paying high interest rates and racking up big debts for the future.

In short, it can be a very expensive world. But the good news is that it is completely possible to live happily on your earnings without getting in debt and without forfeiting what you need. In fact, *A Girl's Guide to Money* and a little bit of determination are all you need.

chapter one
bank
on it!

1

Keeping money stashed under the mattress is, these days, a practice confined to the likes of criminals and people over 90. For the rest of us, the right current account will represent the heartbeat of our finances...and that's something you can bank on.

time for an
account?

If, to you, the term 'personal finance' means an old bank book from the early 1990s, it's time to get up to date with a current account.

There are hundreds of these accounts to choose from so be sure to opt for one that is right for you.

the personal touch

If you value face-to-face contact, look at opening one of the current accounts offered by a bank situated close to your home or workplace.

phone or internet?

If you like to talk your finances through on the phone, there are several telephone banks to choose from. And if you are a time-poor Internet junkie, why not do everything online?

Take a look at the different kinds of current accounts before deciding which one is for you:

basic bank account:

This will provide you with a cash card to take money out of the ATM. It might also allow you to operate direct debits and standing orders but you won't be able to go overdrawn. Interest paid is either zero or minimal.

current account:

This account offers a cash card and debit card in one – meaning you can use the ATM to withdraw cash or hand the card over the counter to pay. You will also be issued with a cheque book. You can set up direct debits and standing orders and may qualify for an overdraft. Nearly all current accounts allow customers to bank online or by telephone or in a branch if the bank has one. Interest paid is usually minimal.

premier or premium accounts:

These types of accounts come in lots of different variations. To qualify you will need a minimum monthly income. Rates of interest are higher, but there is a monthly charge just to have the account.

age-old issues

*B*ank accounts are for everybody. The one you qualify for, though, will depend first on your age, then on your status and income.

under 18?

If you are under 18 and want a debit card, the account will usually need to be linked to that of your parents. But if the chance of this lies anywhere between unlikely and impossible, you'll have to accept a card that allows you to draw out cash from the ATM, but not make purchases. Anything else, such as a cheque book, will have to wait until your 18th birthday.

18 and over

This is when you qualify for a fully fledged current account. It will offer a cheque book and a card that you can use at the ATM or over the counter. There are usually no charges if you stay in credit. You can also apply for an overdraft on your current account, which – for a set rate of interest – will cover any overdrawn transactions by no more than you have agreed. If you do exceed your overdraft by any means, you will be charged a hefty fee per transaction.

TOP TIP!

If you are at college there is a range of more sympathetic student current accounts designed to reduce the pain of temporary poverty while you study. With one of these you can benefit from loans with deferred interest as well as a guaranteed overdraft and minimum balance requirements.

opening your account

Once you have found the current account that's right for you and your circumstances, you've done the hard work.

Banks ask for slightly different personal details, but generally this is the process of opening a current account with an online bank:

CHECKLIST!

1   Log onto the bank's website. ☐

2   Fill in the application online. (You will need your address and previous addresses, employer's details, date of birth, current banking details etc.) ☐

3   Email the application form to the bank. ☐

4   Receive a paper agreement to sign by post ('electronic' signatures are not yet valid). ☐

5   Send this back and the account is opened. ☐

6   If your credit score is low, further checks may be made by the bank by email, telephone or post. ☐

But if you feel more comfortable going in to a branch, put the following in a large envelope under your arm:

1. Two forms of identification. At least one should be a photo ID, for example your passport.

2. Proof of your address, for example, a utility bill.

3. A minimum deposit, usually £1.

Once this is all in order and your card is activated, you are ready to go.

TOP TIP!

Take a deep breath and tell yourself you are on the starting blocks to life-long financial control. This is your chance to start as you want to go on.

the ins and outs of
your account

If you look past the design of your debit card and cheque book, no two current accounts in the world will look the same.

Different amounts go in and out on different days and at different frequencies. It can all be a bit of a balancing act so now is the time to organise your current account to work around you.

FIRST, COME TO GRIPS WITH THE TERMS:

BACS transfers:

Money that is paid directly into your current account is usually known as a BACS transfer. Unfortunately, most people only have one of these hitting their account each month and that is wages for a gruelling month's work!

direct debits:

More unfortunate still is the fact that for each direct deposit, there will be several direct debits. These are specific amounts of money that are set up to leave your account on the same day every month to cover rent or mortgage and utility bills, for example.

standing orders:

These are also expenditures but used to pay more voluntary commitments, such as another personal account.

TOP TIP!

Remember your account is your own. As the account holder you are the only person that can set up, change or cancel any of the above transactions.

first things first

*T*o organise what will be the monthly core activity of your current account, the first thing you will need to do is total up your fixed income and expenditures each month.

Your list might look something like this:

money in!

Take-home pay from work:	£1300
TOTAL INCOME:	£1300

money out!

Rent/mortgage:	£400
House insurance:	£40
Car insurance:	£50
Gym:	£40
Savings:	£100
Long-term budget:	£75
TOTAL EXPENDITURES:	£705

Now it's time to schedule the dates of your expenditures around your direct deposit. Try to ensure all payments come out on the same day...and choose this day according to when you get paid.

the dating game

Although it's not good to be paid in week one of the month and have your direct debit payments in Week Three, you also don't want your account to be debited right on pay day as you run a small risk of your wages not arriving in time. So, for example, if you get paid on Day One of the month, organise your bills to go out on Day Two. Then when you reach Day Three, you are safe in the knowledge that the rest of the money can be labelled 'Me'.

it's money girl,
but not as we know it

If your finances were to stay constantly in the black (in other words, in credit), this book would be half the size and half as popular.

But let's face it – borrowing money these days is as tempting as it is easy. Before you make any decisions though, come to grips with your different credit options and remember they all have one thing in common – the money is not yours!

'It's not a straightforward case of "credit is bad". It is only mismanaging or relying on

credit cards:

To be approved for a credit card – or any other form of credit – your credit rating will be looked at first. If this is good, you'll be given a spending limit, which will be set according to your earnings and outgoings. It will also factor in other credit agreements.

beware!

Credit cards carry two main dangers. Interest rates can be very high and there is no set time frame over which to pay the balance back. So although you will have to repay at least the interest each month, you could still be maxed out on your limit 10 years from now. Look at credit cards that come with zero interest for a certain time. If you keep transferring your balance while closing the old account, you could escape ever paying a penny above the cost of your purchases.

store cards:

These work the same way as credit cards although you can only spend on them in one store – or sometimes a group of stores.

beware!

Sales clerks often introduce their cards to you with the question: 'Would you like to save 10 per cent on this item today?' Your answer should be 'No'. Their interest rates are phenomenal and any mention of a 'saving' is misleading. What's more likely is you'll end up paying for the item 10 times over.

TOP TIP!

The difference between the amount you borrow and the total amount you repay on a loan with interest can be huge. So do your sums first – that credit might not look so appealing...

overdrafts:

This is the name for the credit available on your current account. To use it means your current balance will be less than zero.

beware!

With most current accounts the bank will levy a charge if you go over your agreed limit. You may also have to pay interest on the debit balance.

personal loans:

This is a set amount of money that you apply to borrow from a bank or loan company. You agree to repay the loan over a certain time frame – say five years – at a given interest rate. The money is then deposited into your current account.

beware!

If a loan is deemed 'flexible', it means you are able to re-borrow back to your limit at any time, leaving you going around in circles. Hefty charges can also be applied for paying the loan off in full.

you are **the boss**

*I*t's *up to you to control your finances, and this relies on regular monitoring.*

Traditionally, current accounts as well as credit cards come with a monthly statement that is sent to you in the post. But this can often feel like reading yesterday's newspaper.

how often?

A good rule of thumb is to check your accounts with the same frequency with which you use them.

If this is daily, why not monitor your credit cards and current account online? This method will be the most up-to-date so you'll be aware of the exact state of your finances before your trip to the shops!

If you are not online, there is always the phone. Some bank and credit card call centres are open 24/7 so you can call any time for an update. Telephone banking allows you to access all the information on your account that you can online. The only down side to these options to keep on top of your finances is that there are no excuses for not doing it!

keeping statements

Just because you have chosen to bank online, it doesn't mean you can't print off your statements like a regular account and organise them in a file. Having paper copies of your statements from the last, say, six months can give you peace of mind as well as providing proof of identity should you need it for a passport or mortgage application.

TOP TIP!

It is worth thinking of your different pots of finance as a practice for having kids...they all need attention, a bit of discipline and to cooperate with each other!

watch out!

A healthy current account provides the basis for successful juggling of all of your finances. But in case you feel you might drop a ball, look out for the following potential pitfalls.

overlooking clearance times

Not all money going into your account will be available for you to use immediately. For example, if a rich aunt sends you a cheque for £200 and you deposit it that day, you will usually have to wait for up to five days to access the money (and if you deposit it via an ATM, it may take another day). If it's a real fortune you are depositing, the cheque may be held until the bank verifies it is really intended for you. Similarly, if a friend transfers money into your account online, it may not be available immediately.

not having enough funds...

...to meet your set monthly payments: This means you'll rub two parties up the wrong way – the bank and the company you should have paid. You'll probably get charged at both ends as well as risk damage to your credit rating (see pp. 112–113). This is why you should be sure your fixed outgoings leave your account straight after you are paid and all on the same day, rather than spreading them across the month (see pp. 18–19).

sweeping it under the carpet

If it's been a while since you looked at your bank balance, the thought of it might literally make you ill. But bite the bullet and go ahead. After all, you can't improve a situation if you don't know what it is.

damn it, i've been
charged!

Y ou've tried your best but you've incurred a bank
charge. This will be debited directly from your
current account; the bank will inform you of this.

But don't let this be the end of the story.
You can be absolutely sure that the
staff at the bank haven't sat around
a table and discussed your bank
charge and why they should levy it.
Everything is
computerised and
automatic so the only

person who will actually be aware of your particular charge is you. Don't be afraid to telephone the bank and ask about the charge – what have you got to lose by trying to get it waived or reduced?

hey! I didn't spend that!

If you are unlucky, you may see a transaction on your account you know you didn't make – someone may be fraudulently using your account. Don't panic! Inform the bank immediately and it will refund your money (providing you are using your account correctly) and will issue you with a new card.

why might I be charged?

- If you have spent funds in your account that have not yet cleared.
- If you have exceeded your overdraft limit.
- If you have written a cheque or paid a bill online and do not have the funds to cover it.

control 2 yourself

You can keep the sugar and spice, but 'everything nice' is hard for a girl to turn down. In the real world though, nice things cost money and the only person footing the bill is YOU. So control what you spend now and save yourself a lifetime of playing catch-up...

adding up
the costs...

*H*ere's a question for you – how much do a half a dozen eggs cost? What about tank full of petrol? Or a can of cola?

Although it seems absurd, we have all bought standard items like these time and time again without being aware of their price. This is partly because, since the dawn of debit and credit cards, we no longer have to count out money to pay. We just hand over a piece of plastic and key in our PIN.

This approach to spending has to go out of the window if you want to be the boss of your money. So why not take a trip down to your local supermarket and really look at the cost of basic items? Write them down if you feel inclined. You will see that in fact, the same things can differ immensely in price. So by swapping the organic fruit for

regular fruit or compromising on the
'gourmet' yogurt, you could go home with
many of the same items, having shaved
pounds off the price.

comparison list

item	replacement	saving

total saving

unexpected
booby traps

We all have to grow up eventually. And when you get there you realise it's not the picnic you thought it was going to be. In childhood, you were supplied with everything you needed from vests to vegetables. But not any more!

Remember when the most worrying thing about your own budget was that you had to wait a week until your next chocolate fix? And when debt was something complicated and boring that grown-ups talked about? It's only when you become fully independent that you start to marvel at how your parents managed with the amount of money they had.

Here are the top 10 boring costs that, as an adult, you are now wholly responsible for:

1 A 'sensible' winter coat

2 Taxes, of any description

3 Private healthcare and dentist bills

4 Necessary haircuts

5 Maintenance for your car

6 Vet's bills

7 Any tuition fees

8 Glasses or contact lenses

9 Entrance fees – anything from the zoo to the cinema

10 Work clothes

As a result of these expenses, the balance on your account can still look unhealthy even when you haven't got a wardrobe full of new clothes to show for it. Hard to swallow, yes, but learning how to exercise your own financial control is paramount.

the benefits of a
budget

A ccording to the dictionary, the word budget is defined as follows: 'Financial plan for a period of time; money allocated for a specific purpose.'

To take a literal reading of this definition, the only situation in which you would not need to budget would be if you were a billionaire and had an endless supply of cash. Presumably, since you are reading this guide, this is a situation that does not apply so you will need to draw up a budget plan, which will be set according to your income and your expenditure.

Drawing up a budget on paper is as easy as planning a vigorous workout five times a week. But obviously in both cases it's the sticking to it that counts. That's why, before you draw up your budget, it is crucial to be honest with yourself. If, for example, your mobile bill is between £25 and £35 a month, budget for £35. Just like going to the gym, if you don't set achievable goals, it's likely that you'll give up on the whole thing. When drawing up your budget, you might want to start by allotting a rough percentage of your take-home pay to different areas of your life. For example:

sample budget

Item	%
Home (mortgage or rent, bills, groceries, decorating, furniture, insurance...)	40 per cent
Socialising (birthdays, dinners, parties, cinema, etc...)	10 per cent
Wardrobe (shoes, clothes, accessories, coats, etc...)	10 per cent
Debts (credit cards, loans, etc...)	10 per cent
Savings (for everything from holidays to emergencies)	20 per cent
Money for my purse (for everyday costs from a coffee to a tank of petrol)	10 per cent

budget
timeline

*B*udgeting is all very well but your expenditures are not set in stone. Many will be daily, some weekly, most monthly, and others yearly.

While there is no point trying to predict what you are going to spend to the penny in six months time, it is certainly worth keeping the different timelines in mind.

daily expenses:

Sometimes it seems all you have to do to spend money is get up in the morning. So on a micro scale, consider these day-to-day expenses in your budget:

Lunch	**1**
Newspaper	**2**
Coffee	**3**
Travel fares/parking charges	**4**
Possible drink after work	**5**

Daily total _____

weekly expenses:

These can really surprise you since they are overlooked both on a daily and a monthly basis. Weekly expenses, however, play as much a part in your budget as any other type of cost. Consider the following examples when you are drawing up your brutally honest budget plan:

Take away	1	
Cleaner	2	
Food shopping	3	
Exercise class	4	
Big weekend night out	5	
Petrol	6	
Weekly total		

don't forget:

Your daily and weekly budgets in some ways are easier to monitor because you are more likely to be using cash for these items; and, at some point during the week, you will find your purse is empty. If that happens earlier and earlier in the week, you are not counting all your expenses accurately and will need to revisit your budget.

monthly expenses:

This will become the most worn part of your budget since many costs are built around salaries – which are typically paid on a monthly basis. For this reason take what you can from your monthly income and put it aside for your long-term budget. Your monthly expenditure might therefore appear something like this:

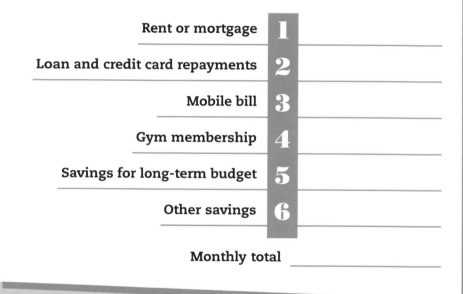

Rent or mortgage	1	
Loan and credit card repayments	2	
Mobile bill	3	
Gym membership	4	
Savings for long-term budget	5	
Other savings	6	
Monthly total		

don't forget:

Your monthly budget is likely to be the core activity of your current account, so it's important to get it right. Schedule as much as you can on a monthly basis to streamline your account – and your life – but note the tip opposite.

annual expenses:

Although these expenses are the least frequent, they can also be the most painful. But if you have put enough aside from your monthly salary, you should be able to meet yearly costs such as the following:

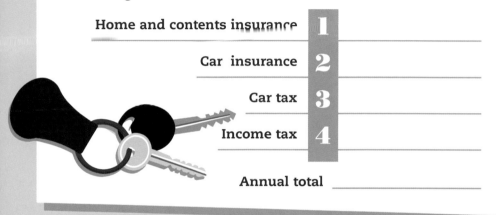

Home and contents insurance 1 _____

Car insurance 2 _____

Car tax 3 _____

Income tax 4 _____

Annual total _____

don't forget:

Note on your annual budget the month that these bills are due, so that you can be sure funds are in your account to meet them. Car tax and insurance are likely to be due at the same time – the anniversary of buying the car – so that could prove an expensive month.

TOP TIP!

It often works out cheaper to pay for insurance upfront each year. Companies make money by charging interest if you choose to spread the premium over the year by paying on a monthly basis.

preparing for
occasions

One thing that is easy to overlook when drawing up your budget are special occasions, which – exciting as they are – can bulldoze all your good work. Plan ahead for the following:

birthdays

As well as presents, these often entail celebratory drinks and dinner. So be sensible. If you are spending a mint on a night out, go easy on the cost of the gift. Why not pitch in for something with friends? Far from being stingy, you are ensuring you'll have the money to attend the next birthday bash.

christmas

This is a pricey time of year for everyone. So before you race to the shops, credit card in tow, establish a maximum cost per gift with family and friends – £15 is ample. As well as returning with more imaginative Christmas presents, you can enjoy the festivities without worrying about how you're going to get through January.

weddings

Tears at weddings should be as much about cost as happiness! But you don't have to buy a brand new outfit every time. Designer dresses are best shared among friends. Let's face it – otherwise they are only worn once. Again, chip in with friends for a more thoughtful present and reduce the cost of hotels by sneaking a few pals in one room...

coping with
emergencies

*B*ut there are plenty of other events in life that you just can't plan for. These can be the ultimate stingers that really bring home the injustice of how much of your hard-earned cash has to go on things you resent.

Your car blows a tyre, for example, or you get a speeding fine. A window shatters, your vacuum cleaner dies or you spill red wine down a friend's new white sofa. To deal with all these frustrating events, it will be up to you to find some money upfront. That's why it is crucial to have a cushion of cash to break your fall.

If you have stuck to your budget, you should have enough to cover

think ahead!

Emergencies are by definition unexpected, but there are things you can do to try to prevent them.

1 Check your car tyres regularly – if you know they are worn you can plan to finance their replacement.

2 Look at warranty and insurance for expensive household items, such as washing machines and dryers. These could save you money in the long term.

3 Have expensive items of furniture protected against stains. It will cost extra upfront but will keep them looking good.

4 Read the instruction manuals for appliances to be sure you are using them correctly and following maintenance procedures.

5 Ask friends how long, in their experience, appliances last to give you an idea of when you might need to replace an item.

6 Make and keep regular optician and dental appointments; tiny problems fixed early will cost less than neglecting them.

unforeseen events such as these. It might be that your 'Me' money amounts to nothing for the month or that you have to blow your long-term budget. But if the costs are spiralling out of control, it is better to dig into your savings – borrowing money is more expensive and should be a last resort.

TOP TIP!

Putting the cost of emergencies on credit increases their cost in the long run and ends up eating even further into your hard-earned salary.

come off it!
I just don't earn that much!

OK, so there are times when your budget will be a simple case of trying to fit a square peg into a round hole.

TAKE THE FOLLOWING SCENARIO:

It's Christmas and you get a speeding ticket on the way to the shopping centre to buy your wealth of gifts. You come home to find the washing machine has broken and realise that the cost of a new one is going to be very high. You are already over budget and have exhausted all avenues that will let you see Christmas through solvent. It's a situation that can get out of hand so short of conjuring money out of the air – **WHAT DO YOU DO?**

Although Shakespeare wrote in *Hamlet*, 'Neither a borrower nor a lender be', he didn't have a washing machine. It's at times like this that you will have to bite the bullet and borrow. But if you have an option of borrowing at a zero interest rate – namely from The Bank of Mum and Dad – that's your first port of call. Don't be proud – everyone needs a little help from time to time. Just make sure you agree to a certain period over which you can pay the money back and buy them a bottle of wine to say thanks.

If you don't have this option, you'll have to pay by credit card or even take out a loan. But don't beat yourself up about this – all budgets must have a little flexibility and at least you won't have to worry about the washing machine for another 10 years.

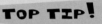

TOP TIP!

Whether you use your credit card or get a loan depends on the size of the bill. If it's small enough to pay off quite fast – within six months, say – your credit card might be the best option, especially if you are still in a zero or low interest period.

payback time:

Draw up a repayment schedule with your parents – and stick to it. Just because it's Mum and Dad doesn't mean you should be casual about repayment. Although it hopefully won't be necessary, you might want to borrow from them in the future and they need to know you can make and honour a grown-up agreement.

budget maintenance

It might be the case that your budget is simply not working. You have tried to stick to it but are still putting things on your credit card or getting overdrawn at the end of each month.

It is crucial that at this point you do not admit defeat, claiming that: 'I once tried a budget but it didn't work.' Instead, look at exactly where things are coming unstuck by writing a list of everything you spend for a one-month period. If restaurants and bars appear often on your list, you might not like it, but there is your diagnosis.

If, however, you have not overspent on anything, look at how much you are putting away. It could be that, in your eagerness to remain solvent, you have forgotten that hard-earned money is to enjoy as well as to save for the future. So don't be too hard on yourself – a healthy balance to your budget means there is less chance of giving up on it.

budget checklist

item	cost

budget [   ]

overspend? [   ]

TOP TIP!

It is often the case that the worse the state of your finances, the less you can bring yourself to care about them. If you surrender to this way of thinking you will begin on one long downwards spiral and it will be 100 times harder to climb back up.

reassessing
your budget

Your income and expenditures will fluctuate as you progress along your life's financial path. So although it's highly unlikely you'll ever be able to abandon your budget, there will certainly be times when it needs an overhaul.

money goes up...

Thankfully, your income usually goes up as you gain more experience at work. You have every right to enjoy the fruits of your promotions but if you know a pay rise is around the corner, don't start counting on the extra cash ahead of time. Include it in your budget only when you can actually see it in your bank account.

...but so do costs

Also remember that salary and expenses tend to end up relative to one another. As well as paying more tax and National Insurance when you get a pay rise, you might decide you can now afford a bigger flat or a new car. So before your extra cash evaporates into thin air, make a pact with yourself that with each pay rise you make at least one improvement to your financial situation. Increase the amount you save each month, or up the monthly payments on any outstanding loans or credit cards.

TOP TIP!

The more money you have, the more you can spend paying off a loan. This will not only shorten the term of the loan, but will reduce the interest payable on it.

example:

Your revamped monthly budget following a pay rise might include the following headings:

Increase in monthly salary **1** _____

Extra to savings **2** _____

Extra to credit cards **3** _____

New 'Me' total _____

'I said NO!'

Whatever your budget looks like, it will involve the word 'No' – and this is often the biggest hurdle to get over. But to remain the boss of your finances, you must remain the boss of your life. Here are a few classic examples of when you should say 'No' – and how:

1

when?

A friend is pleading with you to join her on a night out but your budget that week is already accounted for.

how?

Simply tell your friend that not only can you not afford it, you had planned a night in. Invite her over but do not be moved. If she can't respect your decision, why are you friends anyway?

2

when?

A work colleague has asked to borrow more money when they still haven't repaid you from the last time.

how?

Use this as an opportunity for a 'joke'. Try saying: 'Of course! Give me back the £20 you owe me and you can re-borrow that!' Remember it is they – not you – who should feel embarrassed.

3

when?

You are cornered on the street by a charity worker, asking you to donate a certain amount of money each month from your current account.

how?

Simply say you admire what they are doing but personally cannot afford to help regardless of the amount. Repeat it 10 times if you have to. Also keep in mind it is their job to pressure people. Plus that they won't remember you because over 90 per cent of the people they stop also say 'No'.

danger
zones

T here are times, however, that – although you know you should say no and protect your budget – you go ahead regardless.

This is where you can watch all the hard work that you have put in over the months come undone over the course of a weekend. Watch out for the following scenarios:

you are with someone...

...who is careful with their own money. With certain people you seem to spend a fortune. Be prepared for this in advance – don't be embarrassed to say if it is not your turn or to ask for half of the cab fare. If you go out with that 'set amount', you can also say that you have run out of money.

you are miserable

Just like having that extra slice of chocolate cake, buying those shoes if you can't afford to will only make you feel more down. See the cloud coming and be prepared to fight the urge.

you are already overdrawn

Somehow, money in your pocket seems worth more than the money available on credit. In fact, it is worth just the same. Keep away from the 'drop in the ocean' attitude that occurs when the less money you have, the more inclined you are to spend.

you are trying to make friends

When you first go to college or start a new job, it's tempting to spend more on nights out in an attempt to be liked. But there is no such thing as a 'quick fix' friend, even if you are at the bar all night buying the drinks. So don't bother – it's a waste of time and money.

you are drunk!

After a few white wines, it's easy to pull notes out of your purse like they are nothing but paper. Go out with a set amount and go home when it is gone.

on top of it all

Although budgeting seems like a lot of hard work, the rewards you will reap are priceless. When you feel in control of your finances, you'll also feel on top of other areas of your life, including your work and relationships. Being solvent and having some money to fall back on is also empowering. It means you are 100 per cent independent and a girl who can afford to make her own decisions...because owing no one means answering to no one.

chapter three
shop
until you stop

3

Shop windows seem to emit a magnetic draw to us girls. To walk past without stopping – and then to resist the urge to venture inside – takes a huge amount of pull in the opposite direction. But the good news is you can cure this addiction in a few easy stages...and still be happy at the end of the day.

STAGE ONE:
don't believe
the hype

M ost young women care a great deal about their appearance – to the absolute delight of fat-cat advertising executives around the world.

After all, it means that any product from cellulite remover to anti-wrinkle cream to diet books to stay-on-all-night lipsticks are pretty easy to sell. Simply give the item a trendy image, show a beautiful model using it on television, and then tell lots of impressionable young women that they also need this product to look good. The first stage of coming to grips with your shopping addiction it to realise that this is absolute nonsense!

TOP TIP!

If you ever get fed up with questioning yourself each time you want to splurge on a gimmicky beauty product, smile and remind yourself it's 'because you're worth it!'

get cynical

Before you blow your budget on a something
you had never heard of yesterday but 'need'
today, stop and ask yourself the following:

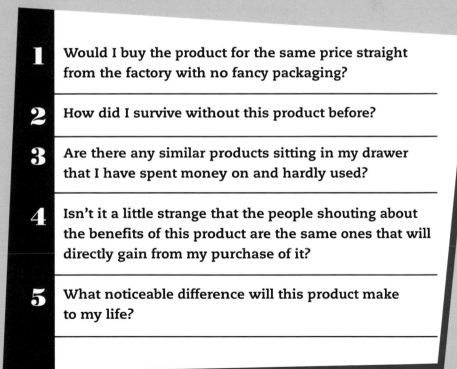

1 Would I buy the product for the same price straight from the factory with no fancy packaging?

2 How did I survive without this product before?

3 Are there any similar products sitting in my drawer that I have spent money on and hardly used?

4 Isn't it a little strange that the people shouting about the benefits of this product are the same ones that will directly gain from my purchase of it?

5 What noticeable difference will this product make to my life?

STAGE TWO:

sensible shopping

*F*or the times you do shop, it is imperative that you do it pragmatically if you want to keep on top of your budget. Consider the following steps to the art of sensible shopping…

spending less for the same

First, don't spend more than is necessary. Keep at the forefront of your mind that there is a wide range of price tags for either the same item or a similar one. For example, these days there are a wealth of designer outlets and discount stores that sell would-be expensive clothes, shoes, bags and even sports gear for a fraction of the price they retail for in other stores. OK, so it might be last season's stock but who is really going to know? And more to the point, who is really going to care?

prices vary enormously

Although sometimes it is satisfying to spend lots of money on a quality product, if it is a one-season-only look you want, why bother breaking the bank? Fashion changes so quickly that by the time your cheap T-shirt starts falling apart, it will be old news anyway.

TOP TIP!

Break down your purchases into categories of long and short term. Spend more on long-term items and less on short-term.

comparison list

item	this season	last season
trousers	£30	£10
t-shirt	£15	£5
jumper	£35	£15
vest	£12.99	£2.99
jeans	£45	£15
smart skirt	£39.99	£17.99
casual skirt	£29.50	£15
coat	£150	£49.95
shorts	£25	£10

Waiting for end-of-season sales makes good sense since you can save up to 75 per cent off the original price.

organize

- Make a list of everything you own, broken down into categories such as shirts – white, patterned, solid; trousers – work, casual, jeans.

- Take photos of all your shoes and stick them to the box, then pile up the boxes. If you can't fit them in the wardrobe, you don't need more.

- Organise drawers so that you can see everything that is inside.

- Organise your wardrobe so you can clearly see what you actually need before you go to the shops and end up buying the first thing you like (see pp. 68–69).

getting it right...

The only thing more damning to your budget than buying too many clothes is buying too many clothes you will never wear. So, before you leave the house on your shopping spree, think about what suits you and what purchases are realistic. This means that rather than throwing money away on a funky pair of shoes that you love for a couple of hours, concentrate hard on some basic requirements. For example, cool trousers but what in your wardrobe could you team them with? Stunning shoes but can you walk in them? Great jacket but will you freeze in October? In short, ask yourself the questions your Mum demanded answers for a few years back – because, frustratingly, Mums are usually right.

buy wise

- Buy clothes for versatility. For example, a plain white shirt with classic trousers is dressy enough for work and will be casual if paired with jeans.

- Set a time limit on your shopping trip and if you haven't found what you are looking for, go home – it wasn't meant to be.

- Take your clothes list with you and don't buy anything that doesn't appear on that list.

- Avoid the 'one for £19.99, two for £30' scenario – unless these are classic items you will wear again and again.

...and taking your time

Spontaneous shopping is the most dangerous form of all. One way of avoiding too much spontaneity is to go to the shops with a set amount in cash, keeping your credit card safely tucked away at home. Having to return home and search for your precious card will give you enough time to make sure that the extra item is within the realms of affordability and that you still actually want it.

And if you want to go one step further, you could even wrap any store cards you have in a plastic bag and keep them in a block of ice in the freezer. Granted, this sounds like a strange thing to do, but it will force you to wait for the ice to melt before going ahead with any potentially 'naughty' purchases – as long as you can cope with a small puddle of water!

understanding cost-per-wear

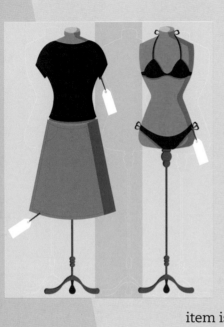

Employing the 'cost-per-wear' rule is another crucial part of shopping. Cost-per-wear is an equation that will tell you how much it has cost you each time you have worn a certain item. Spending £100 on a leather handbag can actually be good value if you use it every day for four years, because the cost-per-wear is low. However, if you spend £15 on a shirt that you wear once, the cost-per-wear is high, even though the item is much cheaper. In some cases then, spending more can be prudent and spending less a waste. It's all about shopping sensibly.

TOP TIP!

Comfortable shoes, classic handbags, well-fitting jeans and work shirts tend to have a low cost-per-wear because you will use them often, over a long period of time. For this reason, it's often worth buying the best you can afford. Special occasion outfits like party dresses or a bikini for a week's holiday have a high cost-per-wear, so paying a lot of money for expensive brands is a bad idea, particularly since they go out of fashion quickly.

cost-per-wear examples

1
One pair of classic designer jeans = £150
Wear them four times a week for two years = 416 wears
Cost per wear = 36p
Value = 10/10

2
One pair of bright yellow stilettos = £45
Wear them three times before injuring ankle = 3 wears
Cost per wear = £15
Value = 2/10

3
One fashionable winter coat = £175
Wear frequently over one winter = 122 wears
Cost per wear = £1.43
Value = 7/10

4
One designer handbag = £150
Use every day for one year = 365 uses
Cost per use = 41p
Value = 10/10

STAGE THREE:
making the most of
what you have

A pplying this rule of life to your wardrobe can save you a fortune. So before you take off for the shopping centre take a look at what you already have.

Remember, clothes can often spend a long time in the laundry basket or on the ironing pile. There might also be several garments in a heap at the bottom of your wardrobe waiting to be dry-cleaned or some shoes you have written off just because the heels have worn down. So wash, iron, dry-clean, repair and re-heel. Then hang everything back in your wardrobe in a different order. Organise things by colour, season or into categories of skirts, trousers, tops and so on. Then look again at your wardrobe in its entirety and you might be pleasantly surprised that you've got more than you thought.

TOP TIP!

accessorise

Remember that a new look does not necessarily mean that you have to head out to the shops to buy new clothes. Cheap accessories such as earrings, belts, scarves and bangles can transform an old outfit. Even a new nail polish or lip gloss can provide a sufficient 'fashion fix' for the month. So while assessing your existing wardrobe, consider how a few well-chosen accessories could give it the renewed life it's screaming out for. You could get your shopping bill down to a fraction of the price.

Accessories are cheap only if you don't go overboard. Go out with a set amount and don't exceed it. If you have any money left over, add it to next month's 'fashion fix'. You may be pleasantly surprised at how little you can spend.

i really need...

You can ensure you buy the right things by filtering down what you want to what you really need. For example:

I want	a pair of red high-heeled boots
I need	a pair of high-heeled boots
I really need	a pair of boots I can walk in and wear right through the winter

STAGE FOUR:
making the most of what
your friends have

O K, so it's not one of Aesop's Fables but in these times of great expense using what your friends have – and returning the favour – can benefit everyone.

As long as all your girlfriends are willing, having a back-stage pass to each other's wardrobe can multiply your selection of clothes by five or six.

Although you and your friends will be different shapes and sizes, things like bags, pashminas, jackets and jewellery often transcend these differences. And borrowing rather than buying can save you all a fortune.

the right occasions

Obviously this doesn't mean turning up at your friend's house before work one day because you feel like wearing a different outfit. But there will be occasions where borrowing is the only way forwards.

TOP TIP!

As soon as your back-stage pass is abused, the arrangement will fall apart. So make it a rule that all items are returned promptly – washed and ironed or even dry-cleaned.

take the following:

weddings

Formal wear is often required here. It is usually expensive and worn just once so find out who has something you can borrow.

holidays

It's unlikely you'll all be going at the same time so make use of each other's sarongs, flip-flops and even bags.

dates

When you are looking for that all-important knock-him-dead number a friend may have the very dress hanging in her wardrobe just waiting to be put to good use.

clothes-swap parties

Let's face it, around 40 per cent of the contents of every girl's wardrobe is more or less unused. Perhaps you were optimistic with the size of some trousers you bought and find wearing them uncomfortable. And because they don't fit, they don't make you feel great. Or maybe that hat seemed like a good idea at the time but now it seems like a different head that chose it.

Alternatively, you might just be plain bored with the sight of everything you can see in your wardrobe. That's why, although the idea of a clothes-swap party might seem a little childish, as long as you are on a budget its benefits are timeless. After all, new eyes on old clothes can give them a far greater life span. And you get to enjoy the bonus of a cheap night in with the girls, too. So invite as many girlfriends as you can muster together in the comfort of your own home, and get going.

TOP TIP!

Don't risk a friendship over an old shirt – in other words, only invite friends you know are going to play fair in terms of swapping clothes of equal value. If you feel you're being offered an unfair trade, you can always say no.

checklist...

What you will need for your clothes-swap party:

1 A minimum of four people is best, and if you are different sizes, remember it is not just clothes that cost money – take along your accessories too.

2 Drinks. A fundamental requirement of any good party.

3 An empty house. A clothes-swap party is no place for boyfriends, husbands or parents. All in attendance must have the same interests at heart.

4 Clothes. Try to all take a reasonable amount – say one bagful each. Remember if you don't see anything you like you don't have to swap.

STAGE FIVE:
overcoming
sale seduction

Shops would have us believe that the idea of a sale is to save customers' money. Actually, the real purpose of a sale is to make the shop more money.

Not only do shops still net way more than they actually pay for the garments from the manufacturers – even when sold at a reduced price – but sales are often used to sell off last season's merchandise, which would have to be disposed of anyway.

In addition, shops actually take advantage of their sales by bringing in cheap odds and ends that they would not normally stock, tagging them with a 'reduced' price and selling them along with all the other remains. So just because you see something with a red 'reduced' label on it, don't be fooled into thinking you must have a bargain – in many cases, you may not. Instead, revert to the checklist on pp. 60–61 to decide if you really need it.

TOP TIP!

Going shopping without a plan when the sales are on is asking for trouble. The more you drift around the shops, the more likely you are to impulse buy and blow your budget. Buying one item you really need full price may cost less than buying two or three 'bargains' you are never going to wear.

the classic sale trap!

All too often, the clothes that you might be looking to replace at your clothes-swap party are the products of a sale – and this is no coincidence. Not only are sale goods usually second-rate, it is often unlikely you would have bought them at all had they not been so cheap. But such is the effect of a sale that even the most prudent shoppers can go astray. So remember, if you leave the shop with a bagful of 'bargains' you'll never wear, it's only the manager that's happy.

successful sale-ing!

The best way to get real bargains in the sales is to know to the nearest penny what the item costs full-price and aim for at least a 50 per cent discount. Get to the shop on the first day, buy it and leave.

STAGE SIX:
controlling
your flicking and clicking

I *ronically, shopping these days doesn't necessarily mean going to the shopping centre. You can just as easily mail order or buy online. But this method comes with its own set of dangers.*

Firstly, there's the sheer ease of it. Flicking through the pages of a catalogue is quite therapeutic. And if you are bored stiff at work, looking at the latest fashion collections online can seem fascinating. Then there is the absence of any physical cash from the transaction. This can create the feeling that you are not really spending money – or at best that you'll work it all out later.

it will catch up with you!
And with some mail-order products you can indeed deal with the payment later. However,

this means a hefty interest rate and if you miss or are late with even one payment, it's a fast way to damage your credit rating.

Although a shopping website often requires your card details so it can debit your account immediately, it can also provide the option of charging the items to your store card. This is the biggest no-no of all, as the money you are then spending does not even belong to you! So opt for the bigger buzz that on-foot shopping offers and shun the complexities of mail order and Internet shopping altogether.

Beware!

While shopping online at work you are usually spending more than you are being paid to be there.

when to shop online

Shop online for items like discounted books and DVDs where you can see the reduction – and postage is free.

when not to shop online

Avoid online shopping from companies that do not have a national reputation, that don't take returns and that don't allow you to change your mind.

ordering from abroad

The comfort and ease of online shopping can also conceal some traps if you don't quite know what you're doing. Often, when buying goods from a different country, the price you see may not include import duty. This is a cost you have to pay on goods you import from outside the EU. Unfortunately, since you are buying online you do not benefit from the personal allowance that you would if you carried them in your

hidden extras

1	Sometimes you can pay more if you don't become a member of a website.
2	Import duty is the tax that you are charged for buying goods from outside the EU.
3	Remember that VAT may not be included in the quoted price.
4	Handling fees, which the retailer might charge you for dealing with your 'difficult' order.
5	Delivery or shipping costs are the cost of physically getting the package to your home.

luggage. In short, this means you could end up paying tax on something as small as a new bikini when the goods are delivered.

getting it there

Don't forget that your online purchase will have to be sent to you, which often means paying postage as well, so that bikini could end up costing a small fortune. Although you'll not escape duty as it is calculated on the total value of goods, why not save on postage by teaming up with friends and placing one mass order? Alternatively, avoiding shopping sites altogether is even cheaper.

returns

It is also worth remembering that if you change your mind, most companies will expect you to pay to send the item back and it is in your best interest to send it recorded delivery – more expense for you.

TOP TIP!

Be careful if using public computers to pay for goods online. Always ensure you log off and be discreet when entering your details. Also remember to stick to well-established websites for Internet purchases.

STAGE SEVEN:
signing
savvy

*T*hese days it is easy to 'have now and pay later.' You can sport a brand new outfit today while yesterday's bill still sits on a store card or credit card, accumulating interest.

However, according to some stores – often those that sell homeware or expensive electrical goods – you can put your bill on credit and pay 'nothing in interest for the next six months'. Sure, you'll need to qualify to get credit, but then it's easy, right?

Wrong! Until you pay off the balance (which you can do at any time over the interest-free period), you will have to make six monthly payments which usually still incorporate interest. The total interest paid will then be refunded to you only if you pay the total balance back within the six months agreed. But if, as the store is hoping, you fail to pay up on time, you will be whacked with further interest charges for each subsequent monthly payment. Paying the item off over the next say, five years, can easily result in spending double the initial cost of your state-of-the-art sound system. And after five years of course, it's no longer state-of-the-art anyway!

TOP TIP!

Companies are legally bound to make true potential costs clear so always read the contract carefully and make sure you understand it before signing.

the small print explained

Credit agreements are much clearer these days, but there might be terms you are unfamiliar with. For example:

1 APR (Annual Percentage Rate): What the loan will cost you each year taking into account upfront charges and fees.

2 Interest rate: The rate you will pay without fees and charges, which will be lower than the APR.

3 Fixed term: This means the loan must be paid up over a certain time frame.

4 Loan application fee: A fee that the lender will charge to make the loan.

5 Mandatory arbitration: Any dispute will be solved through binding arbitration which you must pay for – a real stinger.

now voyager

4

It's good for a girl to experience as much of the big, bad world as she can. So any money spent on it is likely to be worth every penny. But coming to grips with some finance-savvy travel facts before the plane's wheels leave the runway can make your journey both cheaper and safer.

the shrinking
world...

W hen our grandparents were our age, to travel abroad meant they were either very wealthy or extremely lucky. It took years of saving and planning and they even had to turn up wearing their best gear for the journey.

But today, the world is at our fingertips. As we arrive in our droves at airports wearing comfortable tracksuits, we take it for granted that we can take off almost anywhere – at prices that are within the realms of extreme affordability, if you do your homework on fares and are prepared to accept some unsociable travelling schedules.

So whether you want a 10-day girly holiday, a romantic break with your partner, or a year's round-the-globe trip to search your soul, the good news is that there are ways of doing it without putting too big a dent in your bank account.

...and the shrinking cost of seeing it

The travel industry has become so huge that competition is driving prices down. As well as lots of 'working abroad' schemes – which mean you could support yourself when you get there if you want to – there are also companies that offer heavily discounted travel for students or for travellers under a certain age.

airline online

And there are extraordinarily cheap flights and deals to be found on the Internet. Online companies can often deliver better value to customers since they have fewer overheads – such as office space – to pay for. Always search around to find the best possible offer. The first thing you find is seldom the best.

the right
timing?

Unfortunately, the issue of timing when travelling goes beyond simply adjusting your watch as you come in to land.

When planning a holiday, think carefully about when it is going to fit best into your life. Try to organise any short breaks – whether a weekend skiing or two weeks in the sun – so you have to take the least possible days off work. This is especially important if you are your own boss since time off equals lost revenue. And if you're looking for something longer term, like a year's globetrotting, bear in mind that although a year away probably won't make any difference to your long-term career progress, taking it at the wrong time might.

Whatever you decide, take your time and try to consider all factors, including the financial consequences on your return from your time away, as well as the financial requirements of getting there and staying there in the first place!

it's now or never

Ironically, it's often when you have the least money that your opportunity to travel is at its peak – before mortgages and kids start to take their toll. So sometimes it's best just to go for it, perhaps before you even start on the career ladder. Once you have your travel costs covered you don't need a fortune because the trip could be budget all the way. The real purpose of going is to learn about the world, other people, and of course yourself...all of which costs next to nothing. Of course, it's never too late to travel, whatever your life situation, and the same cost-cutting tips always apply, no matter what your plans (see pp. 88–89).

TOP TIP!

Settling into a career, getting a mortgage and falling in love are the three life situations least conducive to travelling the world. So why not pack up and go before they happen or before you get in any deeper than you already are?

making the journey and
cutting the costs

Once you have decided that you are going to get away for a while, you'll need to be sensible and plan how to do it within your budget, however extensive – or not – that may actually be.

booking the flights

Make sure you add taxes on to the price of any flights you find (as well as possible administration fees) to get a true total cost. You can often get the best offers if you take a last-minute deal or if you can be flexible about exactly what day and at what time you travel, and even which airport you depart from. And again, be sure to shop around for the best deal.

allocation on arrival

If you are going for a short-term visit, you can save money by securing your accommodation when you get there. Obviously this is a gamble but it's one you might get lucky on.

travel to the airport

Leaving your car in an airport car park can sometimes cost nearly as much as the holiday itself, so compare prices of public transport and cabs or, better still, see if you can get a friend or parent to take you.

don't go crazy on duty-free

Just because it's cheap, is it really the right time to buy a new perfume? Wouldn't you be better off saving your money for more fun at your destination?

phone cards

Mobile phones are handy as lifelines but using them from abroad will cost a fortune. If you want to phone home, buy an international phone card. Not only will the calls be cheaper, but the cost is dealt with upfront.

money matters
abroad

Cutting any travel short because of money issues would be infuriating. So it's worth making a thorough attempt at getting all your finances straight before you leave for pastures new.

currency exchange

You will need to change some sterling into the currency of the country you are visiting. It's best to check the exchange rates regularly when you want to change your money since you will get more to the pound one day than you will on another. Also, look for places that do not charge commission on your currency exchange and leave enough time for them to order the currency you require if necessary.

TOP TIP!

Pick up a currency converter from your local travel agent. It makes more sense when you can see what you are spending in pounds – and it might make you think twice before you spend it!

U.S. dollars

Bear in mind that some countries will be as happy to accept U.S. dollars as their own currency. Find out if this is the case where you're headed – you may get a better rate by exchanging pounds for dollars rather than for local currency.

traveller's cheques

When going on holiday, it is sensible to take about two thirds of your total spending money in traveller's cheques. Unlike cash, if they are lost or stolen they can be easily cancelled. Make sure, however, that you sign them – once only – as soon as you receive them. Otherwise, they could be used by anyone!

withdrawing money

You can withdraw cash from an ATM anywhere in the world with most debit cards. Although this will involve a charge per withdrawal, at least your money is being kept safely in the bank (away from any potential pickpockets), and it arrives in the local currency.

using credit cards abroad

Most places around the world will accept a variety of credit cards, so these are invaluable tools. However, pay off as much outstanding debt on your cards as possible before you leave, so plenty of credit is available. This means you can also avoid using your credit card to withdraw cash at an ATM, where a steep fee will be charged for each withdrawal.

the value of cash

Don't always rely on your plastic. You might find that your Visa is useless (as well as embarrassing) when trying to make a donation to a Mongolian monastery, for example. Always have some cash in the local currency.

dealing with your home affairs

If you have existing debt at home that is paid by a monthly deduction from your current account, ensure there are enough funds in your account to cover your repayments for the time you are away. Consider opening a separate 'travel account' so you know where you stand each step of the way. This means no nasty dents in your travel money if a bill that slipped your mind suddenly gets debited from your current account.

using the web

Make use of Internet banking from wherever you are in the world – you should be able to find an Internet café in most cities, so do this before you head off into the wilds. This will help you to be sure your home account is well-oiled and operating properly.

safety first

*T*ourists carrying valuables, such as cash, phones and passports are usually unfamiliar with their surroundings and off their guard – a great combination for thieves and muggers!

To really relax on your trip, take a few safety precautions to ensure you are not just another police statistic.

1 **Don't carry too much in cash:** Enough to cover things like drinks, snacks and entrance fees is plenty.

2 **Use a sensible bag:** It might not be the coolest of accessories but put your spending money in something that straps round your waist. You can often buy ones to wear under your clothing to store valuable documents, like your passport and traveller's cheques.

Pay by credit card when you can: These (unlike cash) can be cancelled if stolen, and if someone is using your card, your loss will be refunded.

 Learn the value of the currency: Holding your hand out to a street vendor waiting for them to take what they are owed from a fistful of notes is asking for trouble.

 Look confident: Unfolding a map the size of a sheet with a worried look on your face is going to make you a prime target for mugging. Buy a handy size guide, sit down for a coffee and plan your route more subtly.

 Use a safe: Most accommodation offers safes that you can rent. Lock up all valuables here, especially your passport and some traveller's cheques.

covering yourself...

You never know what lies ahead when you are at home, never mind when you're roaming an unfamiliar continent. That's why taking out travel insurance before you depart is absolutely crucial. The right insurance will cover everything from lost baggage to medical bills to flight delays. Some credit card companies include travel

what you can insure against

When taking a travel insurance policy, check you are covered for the following:

1 Medical insurance for any doctor's bills, medicines, hospitalisation and air evacuation in an emergency.

2 Lost property, including lost or late-arriving baggage, and lost or stolen goods such as cameras, CD players and bags.

3 Delays and cancellations, including the cost of alternative transport, missed connections and overnight hotel stays.

4 Trip cancellation – if a family or domestic emergency means you can't catch your first flight after all.

5 A 14-day 'cooling off' period if you've made the wrong decision – as long as you haven't travelled yet.

insurance as part of their package, so phone yours to check if you are already covered – and exactly what for. Alternatively, there is a wide range of travel insurance products on the Internet at very competitive rates. Taking a policy from your local travel agent may seem simpler but you are likely to have to pay more.

...and exposing nothing!

With insurance, just going for the cheapest option is not always the best idea. If you are travelling abroad and lose all your money, having a comprehensive policy is far more important. So you'll have to find out exactly what you are covered for and go through the small print very carefully. For example, some policies do not cover delays or cancellations. Others only cover delays from your 'original departure point'. This means that although you would be compensated for the delay of your first flight, it would then be up to you to cover the costs of missing any connecting flights and staying in a hotel. Check the policy for simple loopholes like this one.

TOP TIP!

Always look at how and when the insurance company will pay if you make a claim. It might be acceptable to claim for a delayed flight when you get home but if your money is stolen you need it in your account straight away to continue your trip.

chapter five
rescue remedy 5

People who say, 'Money doesn't matter' probably don't need to worry too much about it. But when you lie awake at night thinking about mounting bills that you can't pay, money matters a lot. Most people with money problems seek too little help too late. The simple steps in this chapter will make sure you don't become one of them...

why things go
wrong

W ith all the good will and budgeting in the world, people still find themselves in some financial hot spots from time to time.

In a lot of cases things can start to go wrong as a result of unforeseen circumstances. This could mean anything from losing your job, to carrying out emergency home repairs, to getting a divorce, to losing a fortune in the stock market. These are all situations that can lead to excessive debt, which can mean late payments, which can lead to a damaged credit rating and beyond…

ostriches and sand

The other reason why things go wrong of course is that – being human – we sometimes spend beyond our means and fall into a state of financial complacency. Then, when you have reached the point where the sight of your finances makes you feel sick, a common but irrational cure is to go on spending and stick your head in the sand like an ostrich. This haven of delusion lasts for a while, but eventually – and inevitably – the guilt sets in, the credit runs out and we suddenly find ourselves running our lives around the search for money.

losing your job

When you lose your job, the most important things you can do revolve around damage control:

1	Don't panic. Re-do your CV, get online, buy relevant papers and journals and get yourself right back in the job market.
2	Don't be proud. Now is the time to ask family and friends for financial help, if needed.
3	Ask credit card companies if you can pay interest-only for three months while you get another job.
4	If paying bills is going to be difficult, consider a temporary job, but keep hours flexible so you can attend interviews.
5	Cut your 'Me' money to zero until you get another job. Your social life can revolve around home for a while.

STEP ONE:
addressing
the problem

*S*tuck in a sticky *web of money problems is not a nice place to be,* so denying you are there at all can seem like a good idea.

But to even start back on the road towards financial health, you'll have to admit you have a problem in the first place – and that something needs to be done about it.

TOP TIP!

Don't approach your parents with the 'I'm not a child' mindset. To your parents, you are a child – their child – and chances are they will be pleased you felt you could come to them – even if they can't help you financially.

swallowing your pride

Your good friends and family could well be the first people to call on for help. Lay out in front of them your complete unabridged financial situation and see if anyone can offer you a loan. But even if it's your own mum who comes through, it is crucial to set down some terms and conditions about your repayments – because fighting over money is a million times worse than just having trouble with it.

getting things in perspective

Even if your friends and family are unable to provide financial aid, just being offered a shoulder to cry on and an ear to bend can remind you that, on the list of life's problems, money has to be pretty near the bottom. Having your life, health, and the support of your family and friends, are the only things that really matter. You will probably always have food and shelter and the days when you would have been thrown in the nearest debtors' prison are long gone. So try not to panic – it will help you think more clearly.

get it down on paper!

This is the worst possible time for ignoring your debts and commitments, so write everything down logically.

1 List your fixed monthly expenditures, including loan repayments; separately list outstanding balances on credit cards.

2 Write down the balance of your current account, the total of your savings, and any other funds you could draw upon.

TOP TIP!

The Internet is a good place to find a contact for a reputable debt helpline. But beware if there is any mention on the company's homepage of borrowing further money, since this is highly unlikely to be the sort of help you need.

somewhere to turn

If you feel that there is no one close you are willing or able to talk to, there is a wide range of debt counsellors out there – many of whom can be reached on local-rate or freephone numbers. Helplines like these are very busy these days, since the level of personal debt continues to increase year after year and the job market fluctuates. The counsellors will have heard it all 100 times before and at levels 100 times worse than your own, so it can sometimes be refreshing and constructive to seek the advice of this outside support.

drawing the line

These avenues of support, however, are completely different from debt consolidation companies. Steer well clear of any 'support line' that is offering money as a solution to your debt problems. Firstly, it is unlikely to be a reputable company, which will mean you have no legal recourse should things go wrong. Secondly, the interest rates charged will be much higher than the normal bank rates since they prey on people's desperation to 'get it fixed'. And, let's face it, no money situation is too desperate to devise your own recovery plan, with the advice and support of a counsellor, family or friends.

people who can help

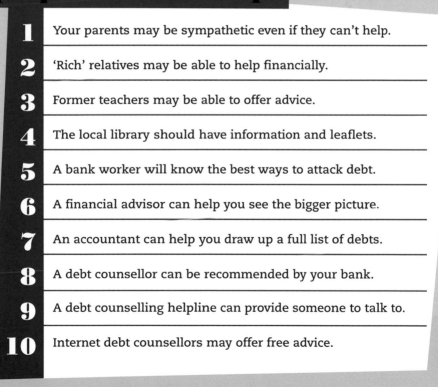

1	Your parents may be sympathetic even if they can't help.
2	'Rich' relatives may be able to help financially.
3	Former teachers may be able to offer advice.
4	The local library should have information and leaflets.
5	A bank worker will know the best ways to attack debt.
6	A financial advisor can help you see the bigger picture.
7	An accountant can help you draw up a full list of debts.
8	A debt counsellor can be recommended by your bank.
9	A debt counselling helpline can provide someone to talk to.
10	Internet debt counsellors may offer free advice.

STEP TWO:
drawing up a
recovery plan

Recovery plans involve being honest and getting practical. Try the following suggestions.

say 'no' to yourself and others

Continuing to shop is not an option. If you can't trust yourself, simply don't let yourself go anywhere near a shopping centre. Also, explain to friends that you are socially 'on hold'. Good friends will understand.

cut up the credit cards

It's time to drop the 'I'll keep the credit card for emergencies' line. Your account is probably now at its limit anyway and further debt is not an option. So cut up all your cards – including store cards – into small pieces, and put them in the bin.

draw up a list of priorities

Otherwise known as 'keeping the wolves from the door', prioritise who needs paying first. These people or organisations will probably be those to whom you owe most money (and who are charging the most interest), such as banks and credit card companies.

draw up an emergency budget

After meeting your priority debts, you won't be able to live off thin air. So draw up a revised budget to cover your other basic expenses. Rent or mortgage, bills, petrol and food should really be the only factors here.

STEP THREE:
taking action
sooner rather than later

If worst comes to worst when drawing up your recovery plan, you might realise (with a wave of horror), that you do not have enough funds to pay the creditors you owe.

It is now more tempting than ever to stick your head back in the sand and wait for it all to disappear. But, at this point, there are two things you can be certain of:

1	**It won't.**
2	**Defaulting on credit commitments spells trouble.**

That's fine, but if you simply don't have the money, what do you do?

honesty is the best policy

Although companies that offer any form of credit appear to set their repayment schedules in stone, this is only to prevent borrowers from being relaxed about their commitments. By phoning the creditor and explaining your situation, you are proving that you are not being relaxed about yours. Don't wait for the final notice before you do this though. The bottom line is that creditors want their money back and they would rather have it later than not at all. You just have to convince them that they will get it and agree to a workable repayment schedule.

TOP TIP!

There is no point giving creditors half the story – remember they have always heard a situation 100 times worse than your own.

"Presenting yourself as a responsible borrower who wants to meet their commitments will get you looked at far more favourably."

what next with creditors?

Creditors will help you, but not from the kindness of their hearts. Their policy is that some of their money back is better than none, so here are a couple of solutions you might be offered:

solutions to consider

1	**Reducing your repayments for a certain time period.**
2	**Paying just the interest on the debt for a certain time period.**

This means that you will be up-to-date with the minimum you owe the creditor, although you will not be reducing your overall balance.

It is very important to bear in mind though, that when you are asked what you can afford to repay, be honest and realistic – however small the amount.

meeting your payments

Set up revised deductions for the new payments on dates that you know are 'safe', that is, your salary has been paid and there will be funds available. Cut down on everything else you have to in order to avoid defaulting on a payment.

keep on top of it

Check your bank balance daily to be sure there are no nasty surprises. This is going to be a long haul, but keeping on top of it now is the only way to future stability. Tell yourself that it will get easier – because it will.

it's not that bad

It is imperative that you fulfill your commitments to your new revised payment plan – that's why ensuring it is realistic in the first place is also crucial. But once it's in place and you are paying your way, you can sleep easy again. Creditors will leave you alone if they are safe in the knowledge that you are paying whatever has been agreed to on schedule.

TOP TIP!

During your negotiations, ensure that when you are able to make repayments in full again, you do so immediately. Being restricted to any reduced payment plan when you can afford more means paying over-the-top in interest.

STEP FOUR:

understanding your
credit score

SCHOOL *might be over but marks for performance never stop. There will always be your credit score that will reveal, in no uncertain terms, how reliable you are as a borrower.*

Your credit rating (or 'credit score') tells lenders how likely you are to repay any type of borrowing. So whether you are applying for a personal loan, car loan, credit card or even a mortgage, the lender will look at your credit file before agreeing, They will do this electronically and instantly using a credit reference agency that holds, but does not decide, this information. The two major credit reference agencies are Experian and Equifax.

what's listed?

As well as your personal details such as your name, age and address, your credit file will list all outstanding borrowing, your payment

TOP TIP!

You should protect your credit score at all costs. If it becomes damaged, it will take up to six years to repair.

history of borrowing and current payment status. The higher your score, the more chance you'll have of being accepted for credit and the lower rates of interest you will be offered.

protecting your score

Protecting your credit rating makes your life a lot easier. You don't want creditors to see a string of late or defaulted payments. This will show you to be an irresponsible borrower which results in any future creditors either charging you a fortune in interest or refusing to give you credit at all.

see what they see!

Your credit score is available from either credit reference agency although, as they are competitors and don't share information, you might want to get both versions. You can apply by post, telephone or, these days, just check your credit file online. Depending on the level of detail you want to view, there may be a small charge. Visit www.experian.co.uk or www.equifax.co.uk for more details.

what will damage my credit rating?

It's not just failing to meet payments that will have a negative effect your credit rating. The following situations might also cause you problems:

1 **If you have not been at your current address or at your place of employment for very long...**
Staying put at one address gives creditors peace of mind that they'll know where to contact you should they need to. And stable employment means regular money coming in, which – in turn – is likely to translate into reliable and prompt payment.

2 **If you have been slow in meeting payments...**
Paying at the last possible opportunity hardly presents you as a conscientious borrower.

3 **If you have no credit history at all...**
It might seem unfair but the only reliable proof for creditors that you will make your payments is seeing that you have done it before. If you haven't, it will work against you.

4 **If you have too many outstanding balances...**
Using credit is one thing but living off it is another. If the creditor sees you have borrowed to maximum capacity, it will be concerned about where you'll go from there.

5 **If there have been too many credit companies searching your file...**
If you are seen to be constantly in search of credit, it is unlikely you really have the cash to fund your existing commitments – never mind another one.

effects of a bad credit rating

Along with regular credit cards, personal loans and an overdraft facility, remember the term 'credit' applies to anything from a mobile phone contract to a mortgage. So in some circumstances, to be refused credit on the basis of a poor credit rating can actually have an effect on the way you live your life. For example, if your rating is very bad and you are refused even a debit card from the bank for that reason, life in the 21st century could become quite difficult.

TOP TIP!

It might be that to improve your credit score, you need to apply for a credit card – even if you don't need one – to prove you can make repayments on time.

STEP FIVE:
realising there are still
doors open

M ost *people's credit problems are pretty minor –
perhaps they have overlooked a couple of credit
card payments or been overdrawn a few times.*

For cases like these, there are still doors
leading to further credit that remain open.
In fact, the sale of loans, credit cards and
even mortgages to the many people
suffering with mild credit problems is big
business, so there's little need to be
backwards about coming forwards.

"non-conforming" credit

Certain creditors will agree to lend to
higher-risk borrowers. However, remember
at all times that they do not do this because
they happen to be charitable. They are often
small companies that operate outside
mainstream boundaries and – quite legally –
make their money from charging high-risk

TOP TIP!

Do anything in your
power to avoid
taking any kind of
expensive, 'non-
conforming' credit.

high-risk borrowing

There are several reasons why you might not qualify for standard credit, but these problems can be rectified:

1	Rebuild your credit score. This is the single most important way to get mainstream credit.
2	Get an accountant to look at your income and expenditure and start to file audited accounts. This is if you fail to qualify because your income is difficult to verify.
3	Play the waiting game. The longer you can avoid non-conforming credit, the less chance there is you might need it.
4	Shop around. If non-conforming credit is your only option, remember rates and terms vary widely.

borrowers higher interest rates than borrowers with good credit scores would pay. Other catches can include a limited choice of options – perhaps you want a mortgage with a fixed rate of interest but have to pay a variable rate, for example. Alternatively, it could be that there is a charge levied if you want to leave the mortgage within a certain time frame, or perhaps there will be hefty fees to take it out in the first place.

STEP SIX:
rebuilding
your credit rating

*T*he first thing to realise when attempting to repair
your credit rating is that – just like trying to lose
weight – there are no real shortcuts.

It's important therefore to realise that the
following tips must be employed over a
considerable period of time:

1 **Continue to keep paying your financial commitments
on time and in full**
This is the all-time greatest credit rating repairer.

2 **Keep credit revolving**
A rolling stone gathers no moss so don't keep high
balances sitting on cards – pay your debt down so you're
seen as trying to reduce the balances.

3 **Apply for some credit**
If you do not have a credit history, apply for a credit card
and pay it off in full each month to prove you are a
responsible borrower.

4 **Do your loan shopping within a focused time period**
Credit ratings distinguish between a search for a single loan (such as a car loan or mortgage) and a search for many new forms of credit, partly by the length of time over which enquiries occur. Too many enquiries may look questionable – as if you're a credit risk to lenders.

5 **Transfer balances**
Consolidating expensive debt and keeping your balances moving looks positive.

don't be fooled

The following are often misconstrued as being beneficial to your credit score but they actually make little difference:

1. Having a credit card with no balance.

2. Paying off balances in full and closing accounts.

TOP TIP!

You can't please all of the people all of the time...different creditors will look for different things when assessing your credit rating, so don't be surprised if one company says 'Yes' and one says 'No'.

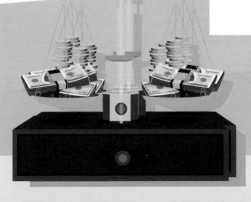

STEP SEVEN:
taking matters back into
your own hands

*D*uring the course of your recovery plan and credit repair stint, you might want to look at additional methods of getting yourself back on track.

Any extra strength you can muster up to pull yourself out of this financial rut will really speed up your recovery process. Try the following options:

set up a new saving plan

No, this is not a joke. Putting even just £5 in a savings account every month can provide a real mental boost.

give yourself a weekly review

Monitoring your recovery progress regularly will ensure you stay on track and allow you to feel pleased with yourself for doing so.

exercise

It won't help your bank balance, but exercising does wonders for the mind. When your workout is done, you will feel you can take on the world.

ask for a pay rise

In today's world of work, if you don't ask you don't get, so get your case together and go for it.

look for pleasure in things that are free!

It's only since the world has become commercial that we assume we must spend money to have fun. But walks in the country, reading, cooking, writing or watching a DVD at home are all great activities that cost next to nothing.

TOP TIP!

Remember that any work for which you receive payment must be declared to HM Revenue and Customs. Take this into account when you are working out how fast you will get back on financial track.

raising money fast

Why not even try to raise extra money? If you cast your mind back to when you were a little girl, you might remember that, in fact, you regularly used to devise money-making schemes. Often they amounted to a bad job of washing the family car or trying to sell your old toys at a boot sale. When the gritty reality of grown-up poverty kicks in, why not revisit that childhood innovation? If there is ever a time when you need an extra income it's now and you might just remember how good it feels to earn some money rather than to spend it.

'Necessity is the mother of invention... think big and small, get your friends involved – they may have ideas that you haven't thought of.'

money-making schemes!

Some of the following ideas might require the support of a friend to make them fun as well as fruitful...

1	Take an evening job in a local bar or restaurant.
2	Do some babysitting or dog walking.
3	Look for freelance opportunities in your chosen profession (but make sure this doesn't lose you your job!).
4	Do some straightforward decorating for a friend or offer to do gardening (if you know what you're doing).
5	Team up with a pal and sell your unwanted junk at a boot sale.
6	Return any unworn clothes to the shops they came from and ask for your money back.

back on track

It's difficult but do-able. Tell yourself that the rewards are worth it – you can face the future confident and stress-free.

chapter six
the future 6
starts now

The future is an exciting prospect when you are both young and female – you can do whatever you want to do and have plenty of time to do it in. But a 21st-century girl has to be financially independent. This chapter explores how to look after yourself and your money now and for the rest of your life…

evaluating your goals

*T*he first thing to ask yourself is what your financial objectives are and when you want to achieve them. Start by categorising your goals into short, medium and long term to get an overall picture. They might look something like the following:

short-term goals

1. To keep within my budget.

2. To increase monthly repayments on my loan and credit card by a small amount.

3. To cut down on unnecessary spending.

4. To stop borrowing from friends.

5. To get into the habit of using cash instead of cards.

medium-term goals

1 To continue saving.

2 To get a pay rise within the next six months.

3 To ensure that my credit cards and loans are paid off in the next year.

4 To tackle my shopping addiction head on.

5 To pay into a pension fund.

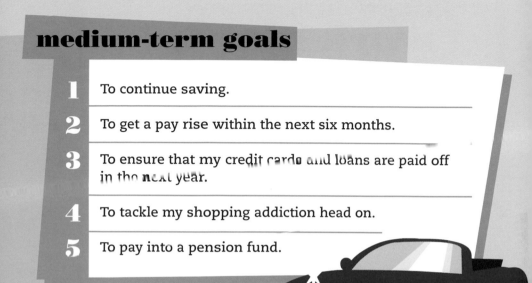

long-term goals

1 To own my own house or flat.

2 To pay off my car.

3 To have enough money to open bank accounts for my kids.

4 To be the company director.

5 To live my life financially solvent.

making your money
work for you

*I*t's widely accepted that you have to work for your money but why shouldn't your money also be working for you? These days, there are plenty of ways you can ensure that it does:

taking an interest

Although it might not feel like it now, interest won't always be something that costs you. As your debit balances are replaced with credit balances, you'll be looking for high rates of interest instead of low. Start by looking at what your current account is paying. None will make you a fortune but you want to see your money at least working harder than it would be sitting under the mattress. Look also for high interest on your savings account (see pp. 132–133 for more information).

TOP TIP!

If you can ever trust yourself to do it, paying your bills online just before you get paid will provide the highest possible balance on your current account at any one time – meaning you benefit from maximum interest.

making the most of technology

Online accounts not only offer better interest rates, but also make life a lot easier when you want to move your money around. This means your money is doing what you tell it when you tell it, which – as well as more potential interest – means fewer potential charges.

benefits of online banking

1 You have instant access to your balance in real time any time of the day or night.

2 Your account is updated faster – you can see an ATM withdrawal within an hour on your computer.

3 Rates and charges vary but generally interest rates are higher and charges lower than regular accounts.

4 If the bank offers a personal finance programme for your computer, you are well on the way to filling in your tax return, if you need to.

5 If you have lots of bills to pay, it saves the hassle of writing cheques and remembering to post them.

packaging your debt

When you take out a mortgage, you'll have to make a choice about what 'package' you want it to come in. Your main decision will usually be whether you want a fixed or variable rate of interest and how long the mortgage is for.

different mortgage packages

1 Fixed rate mortgage: This is set at one rate of interest for an agreed period, so your repayment stays the same.

2 Base rate tracker mortgage: A variable rate mortgage that is pegged at a certain percentage above the Bank of England base rate for a set time.

3 Standard variable rate (SVR) mortgage: This is central rate of interest employed by each lender. It is expensive, so it usually only applies at the end of a mortgage deal.

4 Discounted mortgage: This offers a discount off the lender's SVR. You will only benefit if the lender chooses to decrease its SVR when the base rate goes down.

5 Offset mortgage: A mortgage that only charges interest on the difference between your mortgage debt and savings balance. If you have money, you save money.

6 Flexible mortgage: This allows you to overpay by as much as you like without being penalised. If you are ahead of your agreed schedule, you can underpay.

It is always sensible to take the shortest term possible as you will be saving money in interest. But the repayments on this will be higher, so do your sums carefully. Many first-time buyers have to take the mortgage over more than 25 years.

Whether you save more in interest repayments by taking a fixed or a variable interest rate is a gamble, since the Bank of England base rate – on which your mortgage rate is loosely based – fluctuates. Bear in mind you will pay a slight premium for any fixed rate in return for the peace of mind it offers.

offshore accounts

Opening a savings account in a different country can bring tax advantages as well as complete anonymity and first-class service to your financial affairs. These days you do not have to be a member of the wealthy elite to open an offshore account but most people interested in this form of banking tend to have a strong grip on their finances at home first.

TOP TIP!

Choose your mortgage wisely by considering your own financial situation rather than just trying to 'outwit' the Bank of England: even economic experts can't be sure what's around the corner.

choosing the right
savings account

A savings account is a must when preparing for your future. There is a wide range to choose from but it's not just about the best interest rate – it's about the best rate for the account that suits you. Look at the following scenarios:

'I want a good rate of interest...
...but still need to be able to dip in and out of my account.'

Look online for a regular savings account that offers high interest while allowing you to make withdrawals at short notice without charging you a penalty.

TOP TIP!

Make use of the staff at your local bank branch who should be happy to talk you through the many different savings options available.

'I want to pay...

...a regular instalment into my savings account.'

Some savings accounts offer premium rates of interest on the condition that you pay in a certain amount each month. If you fail to do this, the interest rate will fall...which provides a great incentive to keep saving.

'I don't want to pay...

...tax on the interest I earn on my savings account.'

Although it doesn't seem fair, even the interest you earn on your savings is taxed at the rate of your usual tax code. But individual savings accounts (ISAs) will pay interest tax-free. These will impose a limit on the amount you can put in each year.

'I don't want...

...access to my savings.'

If you can't trust yourself to leave your savings alone, why not take out some savings bonds? These only mature after a given amount of time and pay good rates of interest up until that point.

investing
wisely

Financial investments sound as though they only concern stockbrokers. But the definition of investment – 'A thing worth buying because it may be profitable in the future' – applies to everyone.

For long-term investment options then, why not try some of the following? The sooner you start investing, the more money you could potentially accrue.

buy some shares

When dabbling in shares for the first time, it's good to take advice from someone in the know. This could be a financial advisor, but bear in mind that the cost of this could outweigh the return on your money. For most novices investing only small amounts, the help of a clever friend or the financial papers would be enough. The idea is that you buy shares in a company that you think is going to grow. As the company grows, its share price will rise. A decade ago, for example, investing in a mobile firm or an Internet company would have been a good bet. But beware – share prices can go down.

get a pension

You won't be youthful and resilient forever so what you earn now will need to pay for your old age. The earlier you start paying into a pension, the trendier your ballroom dancing shoes will be in later life (or the more adventurous your senior citizens' travels – whatever your taste is!) so ask your employer about its pension scheme, and take out a private scheme, if necessary.

buy and keep potentially valuable items

Twenty years ago, no one ever dreamed that *Star Wars* merchandise, for example, would be valuable. So, make an educated guess at what you own that could hold the same surprises in store, and keep it (and its box) somewhere safe.

TOP TIP!

An investment is never guaranteed to make money. For this reason a good rule of thumb is to only ever invest what you can afford to lose.

buying your
first home

*B*uying your first home is probably the biggest and most expensive investment of your entire life. That's why it feels as though there will never be a time when you can really afford to do it.

TOP TIP!

You'll always have to pay for some kind of roof over your head, so it might as well be a roof that will eventually become yours.

But rest assured that almost everyone who embarks on that treacherous journey to home ownership suffers financial drought along the way.

But if house prices have climbed way beyond the realms of affordability in the area you want to buy, why not pair up with a friend or sibling? This way (if house prices rise – and they eventually will, even if it takes time) you can get some equity (the difference between the mortgage debt and house value) under your belt, and then branch out alone in a few years. But before you take the plunge, take in the following home truths:

home truths

1 You'll be able to borrow more if there are two of you.

2 The greater the deposit you can save, the smaller mortgage you'll need and the better rate of interest you will get.

3 It's not just about mortgages. Stamp duty, legal fees and removal costs should all appear in any 'affordability assessment'.

4 With a fixed rate mortgage it's likely you'll pay more in interest but you will know exactly what's leaving your current account each month. With an adjustable rate mortgage, you're likely to pay less but the amount can change at any time.

5 When the housing market is robust, making home improvements to your property can increase its short-term value by more than the improvements cost to carry out.

6 In the very long term, it is almost certain that by the time your mortgage is paid off, your home will be worth a lot more than you paid for it.

covering
yourself

As soon as you buy a property, you will be opening up another can of expenses – the most unavoidable being the right insurance policies. As a homeowner, here's the cover you might need and why:

home insurance

This will protect the structure of your property and its contents from unforeseen events such as fire, theft or adverse weather conditions.

WHY DO I NEED IT? If tragedy strikes and you are without this insurance, you could still be liable for a debt on something that no longer even exists.

TOP TIP!

Failing to tell the truth on any insurance application in an attempt to reduce your premium is as useful as shooting yourself in the foot. On claiming, if the details of the application are found to be inaccurate, the policy becomes void and – in return for all those monthly premiums – you receive nothing.

critical illness

Rather depressingly, if you contract an illness that prevents you from working, this insurance will pay for all or part of your outstanding mortgage.

WHY DO I NEED IT? Quite simply, if you are very ill, you can no longer earn money to pay for your home.

life insurance

Even more depressing is this product, which will pay your beneficiary a lump sum of money if you die. If you smoke, you pose a greater risk of dying and will pay a higher premium. So there's another reason to stop.

WHY DO I NEED IT? If you have dependents (in other words, kids), they can use the money to pay off the mortgage and other expenses when you're gone.

mortgage payment protection insurance

This will cover your monthly mortgage repayments for a given amount of time if you lose your job through no fault of your own.

WHY DO I NEED IT? If your monthly salary stops dead in its tracks and you have no savings, your mortgage repayments still need to be met.

realising the importance of
financial control

*W*hether it is earned, spent, borrowed, lent, *saved, wasted, craved or despised, both the purpose and the importance of money is often widely misinterpreted.*

Some people believe that money is the key to happiness, yet one look at the growing number of Lottery winners who end up miserable will prove otherwise. Others are jealous of other people's expensive belongings, but many expensive items are not even fully paid for and their owners can't sleep for the debt they are in. And some people simply say that money doesn't matter. But let's face it – it's pretty unlikely that such people have ever been in the kind of debt that can follow you around like a black cloud.

So what's the best way to deal with this strange commodity we call money?

Regardless of your salary, you can live comfortably when it comes to money if you regard it as nothing more than a useful tool. Tools are for our convenience. We control them. We think of them only as we need them and we keep them stashed away most of the time. If this is the role you would like money to play in your life, then getting it there is achievable.

Remember that designer shoes aren't likely to make you happy for long, whereas forfeiting them could be the start of a lifetime of financial control and peace of mind. So start making wise decisions today.

'Cut down the role that money (and what it can buy) plays in your life. That way you'll be leaving plenty of space for what really makes you happy…'

index

accessories **69, 73**

advertising **60**

addiction, to shopping **59, 60**

annual budget **41**

APR (annual percentage rate) **81**

ARM (adjustable rate mortgage) **130**

ATM (automated teller machine) **12, 92, 129**

automatic bill payments **17, 19, 93, 111, 128**

back-stage pass **70**

bank

balance **27, 111**

charges **28–9**

keeping informed **101**

Bank of England **131**

Bank of Mum and Dad **47**

banking centre **10**

bars **48**

birthdays **42**

bonds **133**

borrowing

clothes **70–1**

money **45, 47, 126**

budget checklist **59**

budget, blowing your **61, 74**

budgeting **30–57, 100, 126**

car **18, 35, 41, 127**

cash, using **32, 39, 76, 94, 126**

charges, bank **28–9**

cheap entertainment **72, 121**

cheque book **12**

cheques **129**

children **87, 127**

Christmas **43, 46**

clearance times **26**

clothes-swap party **72–3, 75**

cost-per-wear **66–7**

credit **13, 21–3, 80**

agreements **81**

closed **81**

history **114, 228**

non-conforming **116–7**

problems **116**

credit cards **22, 32, 43, 47, 48, 51, 65, 80, 106, 119, 126, 127**

using abroad **92, 95**

credit rating *see* credit score

credit score **21, 27, 77, 112–5, 117**

rebuilding damaged **118–9**

website **113, 115**

creditors **108–11, 113, 115, 119**

currency exchange **90**

currency, local **90, 92**

current accounts **9, 10–19, 24–9, 137**

age issues **12**

see also bank charges, maintenance fees, statements

daily expenditure **27, 38, 39**

danger zones **54–5**

debit card **12, 32, 115**

debt **34, 37, 93**
   consolidation **119**
   counselling **104–5**
   recovery **98–124**
defaulting **108, 113**
designer outlets **62**
direct deposits **16, 19**
discount stores **62**
drinking **56**

emergencies **44–5**
express checking
   account **11**

financial control **15,
   24–5, 35, 56, 140–1**
fraud **29**
future, financial **123,
   124–141**

goals
   long-term **127**
   medium-term **127**
   short-term **126**
grocery shopping
   32–3

haircuts **35**
handling fees **78**
'head in the sand'
   100–1, 108

home **37**
   buying first **136–7**

ID **14, 15, 25**
import duty **78**
income **18, 50**
insurance **41, 45, 138–9**
   claims **97**
   health **139**
   homeowners **138**
   life **139**
   medical **96**
   travel **96–7**
interest bearing current
   account **11**
interest-only payments
   101
interest rates **21, 22,
   23, 80–1, 128, 129,
   132–3**
Internet
   banking **10, 14, 93,
   129, 131**
   checking CREDIT
   score **113**
   flights **85**
   shopping **76–9**
investments **134–5**

jeans **64, 67**
job, losing **100–1**

last-minute deals **88**
loans **23, 47, 51, 126,
   127**
   application fee **81**
local tax **78**
lifeline checking
   account **11**
long-term budget **18,
   40, 45**

mail order **76**
maintenance fees **13**
mandatory arbitration
   81
'Me' money **19, 45, 51,
   101**
mobile phone **36, 89**
mortgage **18, 37, 40, 87,
   112, 117, 127, 130–1,
   137**

offshore accounts **131**
overdraft **23, 29, 48, 55,
   116**

pay rise **50, 51, 121,
   127**
pension schemes **127,
   135**
personal finance
   programmes **129**

perspective, keeping
    problems in 103
phone card 89
prioritising debts 107
purse 66, 67

raising money 122–3
repayment schedules
    47, 102–3, 109, 113
restaurants 48
returns 77, 79, 123

sales 74–5
sales tax 78
saving(s) 18, 19, 37, 45,
    51, 120, 127
savings accounts 10, 12,
    128, 132–3
saying "No" 52–3, 106
scheduled transfers
    17
seasonal savings 63
"set amount" 32, 54, 56,
    65, 69
shares 134
shipping costs 78, 79
shoes 64, 67, 69, 141
shopping 58–81, 106, 127
social life 37
    on hold 106
statements 24–5

store cards 22, 77, 80,
    106
student current
    accounts 13

tax return 129
taxes 35, 41, 133
    on flights 88
telephone banking
    10
thinking about finances
    27, 49, 55
    see also "head in the
    sand"
time limit, on shopping
    65
travel 66, 71, 82–97
    safety 94–5
'travel account' 93
traveller's cheques 91,
    94, 95

vacations see travel
veterinarian's bills 35
wardrobe 35, 37, 64, 68,
    69, 72
weddings 43, 71
weekly expenditure 39
winter coat 35, 67
working abroad 85
www.experian.co.uk 113

www.equifax.co.uk 113

zero interest 21, 47

acknowledgements
I would like to thank my
girlfriends—all of whom
represent an entire spectrum
of approaches toward
money—for unwittingly
providing the material I
needed to write this book.
I would like to dedicate this
book to my mother who, I
have finally conceded, has
always been right.